THE JUDGMENT OF THE CROWS

The Judgment of the Crows

Parables & Fables

Steven Carter

Hamilton Books
A member of
The Rowman & Littlefield Publishing Group
Lanham · Boulder · New York · Toronto · Plymouth, UK

Hamilton Books
4501 Forbes Boulevard
Suite 200
Lanham, Maryland 20706
Hamilton Books Acquisitions Department (301) 459-3366

Estover Road
Plymouth PL6 7PY
United Kingdom

Printed in the United States of America
British Library Cataloging in Publication Information Available

Library of Congress Control Number: 2009933437
ISBN-13: 978-0-7618-4820-2 (paperback : alk. paper)
ISBN-10: 0-7618-4820-7 (paperback : alk. paper)
eISBN-13: 978-0-7618-4821-9
eISBN-10: 0-7618-4821-5

The paper used in this publication meets the minimum requirements of American National Standard for Information Sciences—Permanence of Paper for Printed Library Materials, ANSI Z39.48-1992

Once again to Janice

Contents

Acknowledgments

In some of the parables and fables which follow, and where it seemed appropriate, I stole from Kierkegaard the strategy of tacking on a question instead of a moral.

My source for improvisations on Persian and Indian folk tales is the superb *Anthology of Children's Literature*, fourth edition, ed. Edna Johnson, Evelyn R. Sickels, and Frances Clarke Sayers (Boston: Houghton Mifflin Company, 1970).

For the handful of improvisations on Aesop's fables which concludes this volume, I've consulted translations by Olivia and Robert Temple (*Aesop: the Complete Fables* [London: Penguin, 1998]) and by Laura Gibbs (*Aesop's Fables* [London: Oxford University Press, 2002]). The "improvisations" are, of course, original.

Thanks as always to my formatting editor Dorothy Albritton, and to Samantha Kirk of the Rowman & Littlefield Publishing Group.

The Knight Who Saw Things As They Are

Once The Knight Who Saw Things As They Are set out on a quest for the Dragon of Metaphor. When he cast his glance upward he saw stars, not diamonds. When he cast his glance downward he saw grass, not God's handkerchief. When he looked behind him he saw trees, not sentinels. And when he looked at the horizon he saw clouds, not sailing ships in the sky.

After a long journey The Knight Who Saw Things As They Are happened upon the Dragon of Metaphor, and the two did fierce battle; and the knight slew the Dragon. And when the Dragon breathed its last breath, the stars disappeared, the grass disappeared, the trees and clouds disappeared, and the knight, too, disappeared.

The man who chose aloneness, no longer lonely (a parable for kids)

A man in the crowd sees that those who approach him turn quickly and walk away. He looks over his shoulder, but there is no one there; no, it is *he* they are mysteriously repelled by.

The man in the crowd devises a plan. Whenever he goes out walking, and when he sees someone approach, *he* turns and walks in the other direction.

In the end, the man in the crowd is embraced by the crowd.

Allegory of the inn

Two villagers meet every evening at an inn. The innkeeper confides to them that he means to let the inn pass from him to a man who lives in the next village, but that he, the innkeeper, does not wish to tell the cook.

When the cook inquires if the food is to their liking, the villagers, curious to know what he knows, ask, "How is business here?"

"Business is poor," admits the cook. "But the innkeeper has promised me that the inn will stay open."

"Do you believe him?"

"Yes, yes. I believe that he will not sell."

Then the man from the next village changes his mind and refuses to allow the inn to pass to him. And the inn remains open.

"The cook was right!" one villager says.

"The cook was wrong!" the other says.

In his heart, one villager is happy that the cook was right.

In his heart, the other villager is happy that the cook was wrong.

The man in the next village is God.

The innkeeper is Christ.

The cook is Man.

The villagers are the two parts of our soul.

The two men from the town of B

A man took a strong dislike to a stranger who lived in the same village. With every word spoken, and with every action taken by the other man, even at a distance, the first man's dislike grew. Years went by, and his dislike became heavy as a stone. The more he learned about the stranger, and the more his dislike persisted, the heavier the stone became.

Then the stranger approached the man who had disliked him for all these years.

"Why do you dislike me so?" he demanded angrily. "I have done nothing to you!"

"Growing up in the town of B, long ago, I was taught to dislike strangers."

"Why I, too, grew up in the town of B, and I too was taught to dislike strangers!" said the other.

The two men who disliked each other walked off, arm in arm.

The jasmine, the owl, and the stars

Is jealousy most disappointed, not when right, but when wrong?

One night a jasmine said to another,

"Look above you, dear friend. The stars are a field of white and yellow flowers. They are so beautiful that they must be fragrant too!"

"As are we, dear friend!"

"But perhaps they are *more* fragrant than we," the other ventured.

"Yes, no doubt!" nodded the first in a bitter tone.

And they spoke bitterly and constantly of their jealousy of the stars. Then, one dark night, an owl swooped down and laughed.

"Fools!" he sneered. "The stars are not flowers, nor are they fragrant. They are consumed by fire, as *you* are consumed by jealousy." And he flew off.

Yet the bitterness of the flowers swelled and swelled, that the stars are not flowers, nor are they fragrant.

The two women

Is despair, too, an object of love?

A woman wept upon being betrayed by her lover.

"Certainly he is not worth weeping over," a friend objected scornfully. "Please forget him and live your life. You will find another, I assure you!"

"Oh, I am not weeping over being betrayed," the woman wiped her eyes. "That time is in the past. I am weeping for that time in the future when I shall have no cause to weep!"

The mountain-climber

Stone or air?

A man climbed a mountain in the clouds. When he emerged from the clouds and returned to the valley, a friend said to him scornfully,

"But it is a mountain of air, as you well know!"

"Ah, it makes no difference whether the mountain is of air or of stone. It is a mountain in the clouds!"

The lesson of the master

The first disciple said to the master,
"I have caused something wonderful to happen to me."
The master said,
"No."
The second disciple said to the master,
"My friend has caused something wonderful to happen to me."
The master said,
"No."
The disciples said,
"What, then, ought we to say?"
The master replied,
"Something wonderful has happened to me."

The happily hapless gods

Three men of Corinth crossed Mt. Parnassus to the Oracle of Delphi.

"Why are you of so little use in bringing order to the world of men?" they complained to the gods.

The priestess of Apollo laughed and replied scornfully,

"You, who send the sheriff's men into the streets that prostitution in your town may cease, dare to ask *this* of the gods?"

The gallows

Should the punishment precede the crime?

It is told that Roman masters kept a whip in the hall to remind slaves of punishment which would befall them should they transgress. Thus a gallows was erected in our town to remind us of the fate which might befall us should we break the law. But for the Roman slaves and for the people of our town, the threat of punishment was, as one might say, worse than the punishment itself, for it was lived with day and night; but the punishment itself lasted but a few moments, then ceased to be!

It isn't known how the slaves comported themselves with the whip in the hall, but in our town, once the gallows was erected, crime prospered; until, in the end, the gallows was removed.

The actor who was true to his prompter

Where ought Truth to end?

Every actor requires the prompter to be true when he, the actor, cannot be, and a comedic actor of our town was no exception. And, because for this actor Truth on stage was be-all and end-all, he whispered the words to the audience in the same way that the prompter had whispered to him. The audience couldn't understand his words, and booed and hissed.

The comedic actor who had been so faithful to Truth left the stage in tears.

The master and the disciple

"*I was hungry, and ye gave me meat.*"

A master fasted. A disciple, frightened by the thinness of the master, brought him meat.

"You are cruel to do this," said the master, leaving the meat untouched.

"I am sorry, Master," said the disciple.

"And you are compassionate to do this," said the master, still leaving the meat untouched.

"I am sorry, Master," said the disciple, beginning to weep. "But what shall I do?"

"*You* may eat of the meat," the master said. "The hunger is God's blessing. And the meat is God's blessing."

"Are we equally blessed, Master?"

"We are equally blessed."

The man who died of a mysterious illness (a fable for kids)

Is death, then, a dream?

A man passed the hours of the night in slumber so voluptuous that he cherished the life of his dreams and shunned the hours of the day. Bathing in ponds of dream, he awoke cleansed; sleeping on sands of dream, he awoke refreshed; feasting on strange fruits of dream, he awoke satisfied; breathing jasmine-scent of dream, he awoke to a room all perfumed.

When he walked through the town, morose and unhappy, he would speak to no one but his friends. His daydreams were of the ponds, the sands, the fruits, and the jasmine of nights before.

Then the man fell ill with a mysterious illness. No doctor could help him, and he died during the night. The next morning, when he did not appear in the town, his friends came to his house and found him lying peacefully in bed, arms crossed, as on a bier.

"Look," said one, pointing. "He is smiling!"

The man had dreamed of dying of a mysterious illness.

The Kingdom of the Lizard and the Dragon

Is the popular mantra, "I am somebody!" of value?

In the Kingdom of the Lizard and the Dragon, King Lizard and King Dragon meet occasionally and perform a strange ritual.

King Lizard says to King Dragon, "You are too big to eat. Therefore you are nobody to me."

King Dragon says to King Lizard, "You are too little to eat. Therefore *you* are nobody to *me*."

King Lizard and King Dragon return amicably to their palaces.

So long as King Lizard and King Dragon agree that each is nobody to the other, peace and harmony reign in the Kingdom of the Lizard and the Dragon.

Of knowledge and power

In a parable entitled "The Storm," Kierkegaard tells of a pilot, or ship's captain, who passes every examination with distinction, but who finds that the actual experience of sea-faring in stormy seas changes him in ways no examination could foresee. "Imagine him in a storm," Kierkegaard writes. "He knows everything he ought to do, but he has not known before how terror grips the sea-farer when the stars are lost in the blackness of night; he has not known the sense of impotence that comes when the pilot sees the wheel in his hand become a plaything for the waves; he has not known how the blood rushes to the head when one tries to make calculations at such a moment. . . ."

Now, for the academic who has passed his examinations and received his degree, this sort of thing always happens *in harbor*, where the waves are calm and the stars are bright. Unlike Kierkegaard's sea-captain, he has, or thinks he has, a fond conception of "the change that takes place in the knower when he has to apply his knowledge." Of course the academic feels this way because he wishes knowledge to give him power over his fellows, as the waves in the open sea have power over the captain.

In this the academic is usually successful, always shameless.

The mysterious church bell

The people of a village heard a church bell ringing somewhere in the distance, but where? It couldn't have come from the village church, for they heard the mysterious bell on every day but Sunday, the only day when the village church bell was not stilled.

They flocked into the countryside, each in search of the mysterious bell. Some heard it here, some heard it there, but the bell was never found.

Soon each wandering villager fell down on his knees and worshipped the point in the air where he heard the mysterious bell. And the village church was deserted and its bell silenced forever, for the villagers rested on the seventh day.

The two secrets

Once there was a cruel emperor who was also unhappy. He said to his courtiers,

"Roam the kingdom until you find a happy man, and bring him to me. I wish to know his secret. Now, go!"

And the courtiers, who well knew their fate if they failed in their quest, roamed the kingdom far and wide, as the fabulists say, in search of a happy man. The search was difficult, for every man had something to complain of: poor health, poverty, a bad wife, bad children, and so on.

Finally, in a distant corner of the kingdom, the courtiers found a man with no complaints, wants, or worries. Deciding that he would have to do, they brought him to the palace. And the man looked around him in wonderment at the dazzling splendor of the towers and parapets, the gardens and tapestries, the coats of arms, ancient suits of armor, and flickering torches in the Great Hall.

When he came before the emperor, the emperor sat forward on the throne.

"Tell me the secret of happiness," he thundered, "or I shall have you beheaded."

"There are two secrets to happiness," the man said. "The first is being summoned to such a grand palace as this, to see the towers, the gardens, the coats of arms, the torches—"

"What is the second secret?" the emperor cut him off gruffly.

"The second secret is not being beheaded by the emperor," replied the man.

The lime trees of Carcassone (a parable for kids)

In the beautiful hill country of Carcassone there was a man, known as a fool, who grew lime trees. He tended them well, cultivating the soil, watering and trimming them with great care, and his limes were renowned far and wide for their sweetness.

One day a stranger happened by and asked if he could purchase the lime orchard. The fool refused, but offered the visitor a bag of limes to take with him. When the visitor sampled one, he was amazed by its sweetness, and doubled his price. But the fool who had put so much care into his lime trees again refused.

The next year the fool planted another lime orchard, but here the soil was rocky. Still he tended them, watering and trimming them with great care, but when the limes came ripe, they were bitter.

Soon another stranger happened by and asked if he could purchase the second lime orchard. He had heard that these limes were bitter, but he told the fool,

"I can plough the lime trees under and use the soil for growing rich olives." And he, too, doubled his price.

But the fool who had tended his trees so well refused the second stranger, because it mattered not to him whether the limes were bitter or sweet.

The two magic birds

Is a bird in the bush worth none in the hand?

"I have two magic birds," a wizard said to a peasant. "I will put one bird in the forest. If you can snare it, this bird *will* bring you good fortune. Or, if you like, I will put the other bird in your hand. This bird *may* bring you good fortune. Which do you choose, my friend?"

The peasant thought and thought. Then he said to the wizard,

"I shall choose the bird in my hand."

"Very well," said the wizard. And he put the other bird in the peasant's hand, whereupon it pecked his wrist, made birdlime, and flew off into the forest.

"My good fortune has flown into the forest," the peasant lamented, wiping his hand and wrapping his wrist in linen. "I have chosen poorly."

"But surely you have learned a valuable lesson," the wizard said to him. "Surely that bird in the forest is a stroke of good fortune!"

"I do not know which bird you mean!" said the peasant.

But the wizard had vanished.

The man who lied

In the time of the Pharaohs a man in the land of Ramah thought to win the heart of a beautiful woman. But he knew that first he must lie with her, so the man conceived a ruse. He would tell her he was dying, and then, after they lay together, tell her that he had regained his health, and that they could marry.

"Will you lie with me?" he said to the woman. "For I am dying, and haven't long on this earth."

"Poor man!" the woman said. "But would you lie to me?"

"No, my dear," the man lied, "I would not lie to you."

Thus the woman agreed to lie with the man from Ramah. But afterward she was troubled, and he knew that he had not won her heart.

"What is wrong?" he asked. "You agreed to lie with me."

"Truly," said the beautiful woman with eyes downcast, "all I thought of was you lying in your cold, cold grave, and of me lying with another."

The fox and the fabulist

A fox said to a fabulist in a gruff tone,

"I shall not be a character in your fable!"

When the fabulist politely asked him why, the fox replied,

"As you know, foxes are always being outfoxed in fables, even as fools are always wise and wise men are always fools."

"That is true," said the fabulist.

"But, as you also know," the fox continued, "in truth we foxes always get our rabbits and our chickens."

"That is true," agreed the fabulist.

"Then you must also agree it is true what they say," argued the fox, "namely that 'the predator is always smarter than the prey!'"

"Thus, as you say, fables are not true," nodded the fabulist.

"That is true!" exclaimed the fox triumphantly. "Very well, then, I shall appear in your fable after all!"

The fabulist entitled his fable, "The fox that was out-foxed."

The man who did things right and the man who did things wrong

Are happiness and unhappiness questions of right or wrong?

Once in a certain village there was a man who did things right and a man who did things wrong. For all that, they were friends, and met once a week at the inn for supper. One evening, the man who did things right said,

"You know, my friend, doing things right makes one happy. You ought to try it sometime."

"Oh," said the man who did things wrong, "but I am happy, my friend; happy as the proverbial mollusk!"

"But that cannot be," said the man who did things right, astonished.

"But it is," insisted the man who did things wrong. "I am, to repeat, happy as a clam." He raised his tankard of ale and winked. And in truth he seemed happy to his friend.

Then the man who did things right set down his tankard.

"If that is true," he said to himself more than to his friend, "I have been doing things right for nothing!"

"I have thought so for some time, my friend," returned the man who did things wrong.

The next day the man who did things right began to do things wrong. The next week the two friends met at the inn, as always.

"So, my friend," said the man who did things wrong, "how do you like doing things wrong?"

"I like it," admitted the other. "And now I regret ever having done things right! All that wasted time! Thinking about that makes me very unhappy."

"But don't you see?" said the man who did things wrong. "Feeling that way is wrong if it makes you unhappy!"

"How can that be?" demanded the other. "You said it yourself; doing things wrong makes one happy!"

"In that case, you still must be doing things right," scoffed the man who did things wrong.

"I tell you, I am doing things wrong!" replied the other.

They were silent for some time.

Then,

"Can it be that we are equally wrong?"

"Can it be that we are equally right?"

The two parted ways, never to meet again.

The pigeon-hunter, the beautiful net, and the rich corn (a parable for kids)

Once upon a time a pigeon-hunter made elaborate plans to trap a flock of pigeons. The pigeons had done him no harm, nor were they good to eat, nor beautiful, nor worth much. Still, the hunter went to great lengths to make a net, which he carefully wove strand by strand, a task which took him a long time and which wore his fingers to the bone. Then he roamed the countryside far and wide in search of the richest corn he could find, in order to lure the pigeons into his net.

When all was in readiness, a neighbor happened by.

"What a beautifully woven net, my friend," the neighbor said. "And what splendid-looking corn!"

"You see?" the pigeon-hunter said happily. "I knew there were good reasons why I am a hunter of pigeons."

The wandering mountain

A traveler strode up to a mountain, intent on conquering it. He stared and stared, pondering whether to take this route or that route, until he became unmovable, like the mountain. Indignant at being mocked, for so it seemed to him, the mountain strode away, and the traveler, able to move once more, followed the mountain.

The wise man and the fool

The wise man:
"And what will you think of pleasures when you no longer enjoy them, my friend?"
The fool:
"That I no longer enjoy them, my friend."

No news (a parable for kids)

A village sent a traveler to a city far away to learn of the news of the outside world.

When the traveler returned, he said,

"There is no news."

"That cannot be!" said the villagers.

Thus they sent another traveler.

When he returned, he said,

"There is no news."

"That cannot be!" said the villagers.

They sent yet another traveler, and when *he* returned he said,

"There is no news."

This went on and on, until there was no news in the village, for all that the village thought of and spoke of was no news in the city far away.

The happy innkeeper

What is acceptance?

Once there was a happy innkeeper who did a poor business. The quality of his food was bad, he charged too much for his food and ale, and he was indifferent to the needs of his customers. Soon, as you might expect, this man had no customers at all, and a friend said to him,

"Look at what you have done! No one comes here, and you will be ruined! How on earth can you be happy?"

"No, no," the innkeeper said cheerfully. "I can always work in the village, and make the inn my home!"

And so he did. But he was a terrible housekeeper as well, and soon the inn was run-down and filthy. And of course the innkeeper had no one to cook for him, because the cook had angrily departed when the innkeeper could not pay him.

The friend said,

"Now look at what you have done! The inn is so filthy and drafty that even a pig could not live in it."

"Yes," the innkeeper agreed, "but now, you see, I have the whole world for my inn and my home," and he packed up his few belongings and walked off down the road, whistling.

The friend shouted after him,

"You will make a mess of the world, too, my friend, wait and see!"

"No, no," shouted the innkeeper over his shoulder. "The world is much too big for that, my friend."

"Then it will make a mess of you!"

"*And whose fault will that be?*" called the innkeeper, cheerful as ever.

He disappeared over the horizon, whistling.

The mouse and the cowardly man

At an inn in the village of P, two men conversed over a plate of cheese and sweetmeats and tankards of ale.

One said,

"Is it true what the ancients say, that fortune favors the bold?"

"No," said the other. "That is not true, my friend."

Just then a mouse jumped up on the table and squeaked at the other, who shrieked and fell backward in his chair. Frightened as well, the poor mouse ran off.

"You see?" the other said, getting up and dusting himself off. "It is good fortune that I was born cowardly, or that cursed mouse might have bitten me and eaten my cheese."

The mouse and the doorknob

A mouse decided that he would enter the next room like the master of the house. He carefully stacked up books and boxes, scampered up the stack, turned the door-knob, and triumphantly entered the next room. Then, leaping onto a chair and from the chair onto the floor, he carefully stacked up books and boxes, scampered up the second stack, and closed the door behind him. Thus he was a very proud mouse.

But another mouse said to him as he worked,

"All you need to do is to slip under the door to enter and leave the room, as we other mice are perfectly content to do. What is the matter with you? Why aren't you content to be like the rest of us?"

"No, no," said the mouse, "I prefer to do it the way of the master of the house. Anyone can sneak under a door!"

Just then, the mouser of the house saw the mouse busily working with the books and the boxes, and he slinked up to find out what was going on. The other mice frantically squeaked a warning, but the mouse was too busy stacking.

Crouching, the cat waited for the right moment, and then sprang in the air as high as he could. The stack of boxes and books fell with a terrible clatter, and the mouse slipped into his hole in the nick of time.

Awakened by the noise, the master stormed in, saw the cat amid the mess he had made, and disciplined him severely.

Being true to your own nature is one thing, but timing is everything.

The sorrowful prince

What does it truly mean not to love?

Once a handsome prince wooed a beautiful princess from another kingdom, but she rebuffed his advances.

Returning to his own kingdom, he said, "Oh, well, I didn't truly love her!"

But the prince was very sorrowful, for he knew in his heart of hearts that he was being untrue to himself when he said that he didn't love the beautiful princess.

Still, as weeks and months went by, when the prince searched his heart of hearts once more, he found that he didn't love the beautiful princess after all!

In the end, the prince didn't know which was more sorrowful, the moment when he was untrue to himself, or the moment when he realized that, in truth, he didn't love the princess.

The philosophical lamb and the mint jelly

Once there was a lamb who prided himself on being a Platonist philosopher. On sunny days, when he asked the shepherds to converse with him under the olive trees, the lamb and the shepherds debated questions like, "What is the good life?" And, "What is a good man?" And, "Where does one's last duty lie, to one's father or to the state?" And, "Is Ideal Beauty in the mind of God?"

One day a shepherd asked the philosophical lamb a question.

"My friend, have you heard of mint jelly?"

"Why no," said the lamb, surprised. "I don't believe that I have."

"Well," said the shepherd, "it goes very well with roasted lamb."

From that moment on the lamb ceased being a Platonist and became an Aristotelian.

The parrot who repeated himself

How far should we go in being true to ourselves?

Once there was a parrot who spoke his own mind. Unlike his fellow parrots, who merely repeated the sounds of the forest, *he* had no need to imitate the screech of the peacock, the chirring of the monkey, or the hiss of the serpent.

The parrot boasted over and over of his prowess, until the other animals grew sick and tired of him.

"Boast, boast, boast!" screeched the peacock. "Upon my word, all this repetitious boasting. . . ."

"Yes," hissed the serpent. "All you do, my friend, is parrot yourself!"

"Yes," agreed the monkey. "If I have heard you brag of your prowess once, my friend, I have heard it a thousand times!"

The animals departed to their jungle homes and the parrot had no one to talk to but himself.

The townspeople and the birds of the air

There was a well-known man in our town who spoke thrillingly of rare and exotic destinations he had visited. His descriptions of landscapes, beaches, rivers, forests, and mountains were so vivid and exciting that hundreds of townspeople flocked to visit them too.

Then it was discovered that the man was a hoaxer who had never visited these places at all, not a single one! The people of our town were so disappointed in the hoaxer, and so disappointed in themselves for being deceived, that they stopped visiting the exotic destinations that he had spoken so eloquently about.

But the birds of the air, who hadn't heard the thrilling words of the hoaxer, flocked happily, as always, to the exotic destinations he had described.

The magic fig tree

A magic fig tree grew figs as quickly as the villagers could pick them. Every villager ate his fill and took home baskets of figs, and still the fig tree grew figs as quickly as the villagers could pick them.

Finally the villagers grew sick of figs and stopped visiting the fig tree. The fig tree grew very angry, pulled up its roots, and left the village in a huff, never to be seen again! That, too, was magic, but no one in the village cared a fig.

Baldonaldo and the shower of stars

Do the gods punish us for being right?

In our village there once lived a peasant named Baldonaldo. Everyone called him Mad Baldonaldo, because he claimed that the stars were made of glass. He stopped each of us that he happened to meet in the countryside, in the street, in the markets, or in the village square, and said in a loud voice, "The stars are made of glass, my friend! The stars are made of glass!" Finally we grew weary of Baldonaldo, and shunned him, so that he was left alone to mutter nonsense all by himself.

Late one night, Baldonaldo got out of bed, walked to the deserted village square, and began shouting in a louder voice than before, "The stars are made of glass, my friends! The stars are made of glass!"

Baldonaldo's voice was so loud that he woke the gods who were fast asleep in the Seventh Sphere! Enraged, they sent a shower of stars to crash on poor Baldonaldo's head. And he was cut to ribbons, for the stars truly were made of glass!

The next morning two peasants met in the village square.

"He was right," one peasant said, looking down at the pieces of glass and of Baldonaldo. "The stars are made of glass."

"Anyway," the other peasant replied, walking away from the pieces of glass and of Baldonaldo, "I should say that he got what he deserved."

The misunderstood king

A king ordered the tower of Babel to be built, but no one understood his order, so that the tower was never built.

The rabbit and the Amazing Electric Rosetta Stone

A learned man devoted his life to the study of rabbits. One day he said to his friends, "I will now determine if rabbits possess a language that humans can understand."

"Rabbits can't speak, you fool," one objected.

"No matter," the learned man waved his hand. "You have seen rabbits running over and over again their tracks in the snow. I am convinced that this is their way of writing, and of saying something to us."

And so the learned man took up the study of languages, and discovered how the famous Rosetta Stone deciphered the Egyptian hieroglyphic, and acquired many other secrets of translation from one language to another. Even though his friends scoffed at him, he spent many years in his pursuit of the language of rabbits, until he grew old and feeble.

Finally, when he was about to die, the learned man made a machine that he proudly called the Amazing Electric Rosetta Stone, and invited his friends to witness its unveiling.

"How does it work?" one asked.

"All you do," the man explained, "is to insert into the machine a photograph of a field where a rabbit has run over and over again its tracks in the snow. It will translate what the rabbit is trying to say on this screen."

His friends grew excited and urged the man to turn on the machine and insert the picture, which he did.

The machine whirred and hummed, the man and his friends anxiously leaned forward before the screen, and, sure enough, letters of the alphabet began to form, and then words, and then a sentence.

The sentence read,

I AM RUNNING OVER AND OVER AGAIN MY TRACKS IN THE SNOW.

The tiger and the Brahman[1]

A tiger was caught in a trap. He tried in vain to get out through the bars, and gnashed at them with rage and grief when he failed.

By chance a poor Brahman came by. "Let me out of this cramped cage where I cannot even stretch my legs and feel the sun's warmth, O Pious One," cried the tiger.

"Nay, my friend," replied the Brahman mildly, "doubtless you would eat me if I did."

"Not at all!" swore the tiger with many oaths; "On the contrary, I should be forever grateful, and serve you as a slave!"

Now as the tiger continued to sob and sigh and weep and swear, the pious Brahman's heart softened, and at last he consented to open the door of the cage.

"What a fool you are!" exclaimed the tiger. "What is to prevent my eating you now?"

The Brahman jumped in the cage and held the door shut so the tiger could not open it. After trying to get at the Brahman, the tiger walked a short distance and lay down in the warm sun, stretching and yawning.

And the Brahman was happy to be safe, and the tiger happy to be free.

Trapped or hungry, be happy with what you have.

---

1. Improvisation on a tale from the *Panchatantra.*

The poor man and the flask of oil[2]

Once there was a poor man who lived next to a wealthy merchant. As the merchant was a kind neighbor, he one day sent a flask of rich oil to the poor man. The poor man was delighted, and put it carefully away on the top shelf. One evening, as he was gazing at it, he said aloud, "I wonder how much oil there is in that bottle. There is a huge quantity. If I sold it, I could buy five sheep. Every year I should have lambs, and before long I should have a flock. Then I could sell some of the sheep, and be rich enough to marry a wife. And perhaps we would have a son. And what a fine boy he would be! So, tall, strong, and obedient! But if he should disobey me," and he angrily raised the staff which he held in his hand, "I should punish him thus."

And the poor man appeased his anger by swinging the staff over his head and bringing it heavily to the ground, narrowly missing the flask of oil on the shelf.

And the poor man sold the flask, acquired a flock of sheep, a wife, and a fine son.

The next time someone says that you can't have your cake and eat it too, don't listen.

---

2. Improvisation on a tale from the *Panchatantra*.

The seeds and the wheat[3]

A man entered a field of wheat and reaped some of the ripe grain. The owner of the field demanded why he had stolen the wheat. The thief replied,

"My Lord, I have not stolen any wheat belonging to you. You planted only the seeds, and what I reaped was the ripe wheat. Why do you call me a thief?"

To resolve the dispute, the two men went before a judge.

"Which of us is right, and which is wrong?" they asked.

The judge sighed,

"There is just no telling, my friends. Therefore *I* will claim the wheat, for *I* have neither sown nor reaped it."

You don't always reap what you sow.

3. Improvisation on a Persian fable.

Legend of the missing brother

In a far mountain country an Indian chief called Tall Cliff had two strong and handsome sons: Heavy Stone and Falling Rocks. Falling Rocks, the older, was the favorite of Tall Cliff. The two brothers went hunting in the mountains every day, and brought much bounty to their father's lodge—beaver, squirrel, wild turkey, deer, and opossum.

One day, Heavy Stone returned alone and weeping from the mountains and told his father that the brother was lost. Tall Cliff, who knew that Heavy Stone was jealous of his brother, suspected that he had done away with him, but he could do nothing but lament and bid Heavy Stone to go into the mountains every day to look for his brother. When Tall Cliff lay dying, he asked Heavy Stone to promise to keep looking for his brother, and Heavy Stone gave his promise, for he had a good heart after all, and had done his brother no harm.

To this day, when you travel in the mountain country, you can see Indian signs made by Heavy Stone, the younger son of Tall Cliff: WATCH OUT FOR FALLING ROCKS.

What you see is not always what you get.

The master and the disciple

The disciple: "Thank you, master, for your wisdom!"

The master: "True humility is to refuse all compliments. Difficult to do, since the only way to be unworthy of compliments is to return them!"

The poor teacher

The lion lay down with the lamb. The lamb said, "Teach me how to be a lion." The lion devoured him. Then, a muffled voice: "I am waiting."

The unhappy emperor

An unhappy emperor, anxious to know what his subjects think of him, leaves the palace in disguise and roams the streets. In cafes he hears whispers, and shouts on street corners and in parks, "Down with the emperor! The emperor is a swine!" and so forth. And in time he becomes one of the whispering and shouting public throng, and knows happiness for the first time.

The emperor removes his disguise. No one in cafes and parks or on street corners recognizes him. And he is unhappy once more.

The revolt of the marionettes

Where may rebellion end and acceptance begin?

Once there was a marionette named Luigi who grew tired of having his strings pulled.

"My friends," he said to his fellow marionettes, "the time has come to revolt and leave the house of our master Leon Batista. Will you join me on the open road as we march to freedom?" And he pulled off his strings to show them that he was very serious.

"But we are afraid to pull off our strings," said the other marionettes, for they were more timid than Luigi, and well accustomed to their strings. "Still, we would like to join you on the open road. But we do not know how!"

"I will tell you how," said Luigi. "You will climb upon each others' shoulders, one on top of the other, and the one on top will pull the strings of the one below him. And I shall ride on top, pulling the strings of the one below me. Thus we will march to freedom on the open road!"

And the marionettes did as they were told, and climbed on each others' shoulders, with Luigi on top, and they left the master Leon Batista's house and clacked and clattered down the open road, singing. And what a wonderful sight they made! Many a passersby stared at the ladder of clacking and clattering marionettes pulling each others' strings and singing at the top of their lungs.

Finally one passerby held up his hand.

"What are you doing, my friends?" And to Luigi: "Where are *you* going?"

"We are gaining our freedom!" Luigi said, looking down at the passerby. "What does it matter where we are going? As you see, *I* have pulled off my strings, and soon enough my timid friends here will pull off their strings if, God willing, I can give them the courage."

Then the passerby laughed.

"But your companions are wiser than you, my friend," he said. "We *all* have strings attached to us, marionettes and men alike. I am a poor man, and the rich landowner for whom I toil in the fields pulls my strings. My good friend Giovanni is a henpecked husband, and the wife pulls his strings. As for the mayor of my village, the Duke of Milan pulls *his* strings, you may rely on that!"

Luigi and the other marionettes were silent for a long moment.

"*All* are pulled by strings?" Luigi asked the passerby in astonishment.

"Strings you cannot see," nodded the passerby, "but strings nevertheless, my friends! And the stars, the moons, the planets, and the comets, they too are pulled by strings; and God, praise be to Him, is the master of them all!"

The marionettes began to weep, and Luigi wept with them, and they all voted to return to their master Leon Batista. When they arrived, the master Leon Batista wept with them, and threw his arms around Luigi, and re-attached Luigi's strings.

And the marionettes and the master Leon Batista lived happily ever after.

The unhappy bride

On her wedding night a bride, unable to sleep, looks at her sleeping husband. She frowns, and then sudden tears flow down her cheeks. The next night and the next the same ritual, until it becomes an addiction. Strange to say, however, mornings after she feels much better, better than she would have felt otherwise!

Remembering the disturbing streak of moroseness that he had detected in the bride before getting married, the groom notices her increasingly cheerful moods. And he congratulates himself on marrying such a happy girl!

The piebald monkey

What price pride?

A piebald monkey escaped from the zoo. Shortly thereafter, on a country road, he saw a figure approaching him. It was the zookeeper.

"The zoo is warm and safe, my friend," the keeper said. "In the countryside you'll starve, or freeze to death at night, I guarantee it."

"Did you find me because I am piebald?"

"No. You were the first monkey I happened upon."

"Then you are looking for the wrong monkey," the monkey said, and scampered off.

The parable in search of a moral

A parable went in search of a moral. Soon he encountered a traveler and asked, "Can you tell me what my moral is?"

"That is it."

"My question to you about my moral is my moral?"

"Yes. And it is not your moral."

The parable became angry. "You lay traps for me! I still don't know what my moral is!"

"Now that, too, is the moral. As long as you must search for the moral, my friend, everything, and therefore nothing, is the moral."

King Solomon

What would wisdom seem like in a parallel universe where plus is minus and black is white? Not as different as you and I might think!

Two women were brought before King Solomon; both lay claim to the same child; each argued eloquently on her own behalf. Solomon listened patiently, then dismissed them, saying that they would have his decision the next day.

At the appointed hour both women appeared, beaming in anticipation of Solomon's judgment. He said,

"It is my decree that both of you shall be cut in half to make one woman, so that the child may have its proper mother."

The witness tree

A witness tree was informed by angry villagers that they intended to hang a man from one of its branches. The tree turned his face away. After the hanging, he announced to his friends that he had witnessed. They said,

"But you turned your face away!"

"Yes. But it was my branch they hanged him from."

Appointment in Samaria

Long ago, in the ancient city of Samaria, in Palestine, Death made his rounds one day.

He knocked on the door of a dwelling.

"I am looking for Ibn Baksheesh Ben Yusuf," he told the man who opened the door. The man began to tremble, for he well knew who he was talking to.

"But I am not Ibn Baksheesh Ben Yusuf," he said. "He lives in the dwelling down the street, on the corner."

"Truly?" smiled Death, and put his hand on the man's right shoulder. And the man died that afternoon.

Then Death went down the street and knocked at the door of the dwelling on the corner.

"I am looking for Ibn Baksheesh Ben Yusuf," Death told the man who answered the door. He too began to tremble, for, like the first man, he knew Death when he saw him.

"But I am not Ibn Baksheesh Ben Yusuf," this man said. "He lives in the dwelling down the next street, on the corner."

"Truly?" smiled Death, and put his hand on the man's right shoulder. And the man died that afternoon.

Then Death went down the next street and knocked on the door of the dwelling on the corner. And like the other two men, the man who lived in this dwelling swore that he was not Ibn Baksheesh Ben Yusuf. And Death put his hand on this man's right shoulder, and he died that afternoon.

So it went all day long until Death, wearied of his journeying around the city of Samaria, returned to his own dwelling.

His wife made two cups of mint tea. Then she asked,

"Did you find Ibn Baksheesh Ben Yusuf, my dear?"

Death sipped his tea thoughtfully and was silent for a moment. Then he said, shaking his head,

"Ah, yes and no, my dear! Yes and no."

"But what kind of answer is that, my dear?"

Then Death laughed, sipping his tea.

"This Ibn Baksheesh Ben Yusuf is everywhere and nowhere!" he exclaimed. "He is mortal and he is immortal! What strange creatures these humans are, my dear!"

And Death finished his tea and went to bed right after supper, for he knew he must be up early the next day.

The silent students

A teacher is greeted by silence when he asks his students, "Which would you choose? For paradise to be *destroyed*, and to know that you could never return? Or for paradise to be *spared*, and to know that you could never return?"

The pernicious sun

Is doubt necessary to sustain life?

One day the sun rose in the east as always, then set immediately. When the astonished moon asked him why he did this, the sun said, "Because I never doubted that I could. It is up to others to doubt, and to cherish doubt!"

The judgment of the crows

Does the man who despises himself truly esteem himself as a self-despiser?

A murder of crows passed unhappy judgment on one of their own kind. A passing hawk exclaimed, "How can you do such a thing? You, too, are crows!" "Oh," they replied. "Now it is his turn to pass unhappy judgment on *us*. In this way we happily pass the time."

The undisciplined teacher

Presiding over an unruly class of students, a teacher improvised this lesson:

"Self-mastery should always embrace a moment when the self, abandoned to its own devices, is permitted to run wild. That, too, is self-mastery."

The class settled down and listened attentively.

The stubborn lemons (a fable for kids)

A bunch of plump, savory lemons on a tree witnessed the following: A peasant happened by, picked up one of their brethren on the ground and ate it, rind and all, in a single gulp! The lemons said to one another,

"That is outside the order of things. Therefore *we* shall refuse to fall."

The two mad milk peddlers

Is madness contagious?

Two mad milk peddlers sold their wares every Sunday in our village, one setting up shop at the north end, the other at the south end. They each displayed buckets of differing sizes, which the villagers would return to be filled the next Sunday. They both charged the same price, but the first madman poured milk into smaller and smaller buckets, and the second into larger and larger buckets.

The first said to the north end villagers,

"Yes, it's true that your buckets are smaller and smaller," he said, "But you will savor my milk all the more, until a few drops will be the most precious to your children."

The second said to the south end villagers,

"Yes, it's true that your buckets are larger and larger. My milk may not taste as sweet, but there will be more for your children."

One day a stranger came to our village. He said to the north and south end villagers, "But these peddlers are out of their heads! Both of them!"

"Yes," the villagers agreed. "We know that. But we are happy with the milk."

The whispering animals

On the day that animals acquired the power of speech, we were astounded to discover that they had nothing interesting to say!

Nevertheless, we lay awake at night, restless, troubled, straining to hear them whispering about us.

The identical bald men

Two identical bald men sit down at table. Pointing to his bald pate, one says, "On me it looks good." The other agrees, "On you it looks good." Both are comforted.

Parable of the two moons

Beauty is not in the eye of the beholder.

In the garden a master asks his disciples,

"Which is more beautiful, the moon in the sky, or the reflection of the moon in the pool?"

As the master understands, one disciple will say, "The moon in the sky," and another will say, "The reflection of the moon in the pool."

And, as the master understands, *all* the disciples will say, "Master will tell us that we are both right, for beauty is in the eye of the beholder."

And yet the master says to them,

"You are both wrong."

"But who is to say, Master?" ask the bewildered disciples.

The master says to the disciples who love the moon in the sky,

"Ask the moon in the pool."

And to the disciples who love the moon in the pool,

"Ask the moon in the sky."

When all the disciples are silent, the master bows before them, saying,

"Now you understand the parable of the two moons."

The mystic who grew larger and larger

A mystic said to a disciple, "True mysticism does not seek to get closer to the Beyond, but to diminish the Beyond until it has no meaning."

The disciple replied, "You mean—"

"I mean that one must become one with the Beyond."

The two women and the mirror

A beautiful woman gazes in a mirror.
"That is me!" she says.
An ugly woman gazes in a mirror.
"That is not me!" she says.
Both are right; both are wrong.

The valley of decision

Is free will a decision?

Multitudes, multitudes, wish to enter the valley of decision. To enter, however, they have to decide to enter. And to decide to enter, they have to decide to decide to enter, and so forth. In the end they decide to stay where they are. To stay where they are, however. . . .

The yellow bird

A yellow bird flew onto a branch next to two sparrows.
"A canary!" the first sparrow said.
"All canaries aren't yellow, my friend," the yellow bird said.
"And all yellow birds aren't canaries, my friend," the second sparrow said.
"So am I content to be a yellow bird."

The hound and the hart

On the first day of the hunt, the hart sat down before the hound, and the hound went away, disappointed.

On the second day of the hunt, the hart sat down before the hound, and again the hound went away, disappointed.

On the third day of the hunt, the hart ran from the hound, who chased him, caught him, and tore him to pieces.

"I am well rebuked," the hound said to himself.

The Messiah who would be kind

A penitent asks a Messiah,

"Lord, at long last, when will you come?"

The Messiah says,

"If I come, then I am not here, within you. If I am here, within you, I need not come."

"I am disappointed in your answer," the penitent has the courage to say. Yet he bows his head.

"Thus you understand," the Messiah says.

"O have mercy!" the penitent implores, "I do not understand."

"Were my words not sufficiently clear?" the Messiah asks kindly. "*Such* is my mercy."

The all-comprehending Zeus

A contemplative Zeus said to the assembly on Olympus:

"My friends, it is easy to envision Poseidon becoming tired of the sea. It is equally easy to envision the sea becoming tired of Poseidon. Witness, in both cases, the eternal ebb and flow of the waves!"

The not-so-grim reaper

Are the wages of sin life?

The grim reaper appeared at the door, asking for B.

"You have the wrong house!" the occupant assured him. "B's house is down the street, at the end of the cul de sac."

"That's well and good, my friend," the reaper shrugged. "I can wait for *him*."

"But B. is guiltier of sin than I am!"

The reaper grinned broadly.

"Ah, that is why I can wait for him."

New parable of the leopards in the temple

Are false gods true after all?

Kafka writes, "Leopards break into the temple and drink to the dregs what is in the sacrificial pitchers; this is repeated over and over again; finally it can be calculated in advance, and it becomes part of the ceremony."

Let us go further. After an even longer time, the temple congregation begins to worship the leopards as gods, until one man rises and says in a loud voice, "I can remember how you broke in here in the old days; you are merely intruders, false gods!"

The congregation grows restless and begins whispering.

Then the leopards reply, "But we are not false gods. We are leopards!"

The congregation resumes its worship.

The monks of Skellig Michael

What do we wish for the courageous?

In the 6th century Christian monks in Ireland, on hearing news of the marauding Vikings, move to the tiny island of Skellig Michael just off the coast. There they build stone huts and live out their miserable lives in loneliness, cold, and—who can say?—despair and disappointment that the Vikings never showed up after all!

And it is their disappointment, not their courage, tenacity, and the poignancy of stone dwellings on a forlorn island, that moves visitors to this very day; it is, one may say, the spirit of the place.

Or is it the spirit of the visitors?

The forbidden dream

What do we ask of our dreams? What do our dreams ask of us?

In a number of succeeding nights I had the same dream, the sort of dream many have, of wandering toward a destination, in my case a childhood home full of warmth, cheer, and comfort, and getting lost. Or, if not getting lost, then falling short of my destination, perhaps because the sun set and the moon rose and I had to find lodging for the night, and for the next, and so on.

Then, one night, the dream changed, and I actually arrived at my destination. And a voice said,

"This dream is forbidden."

"Why is it forbidden?" I replied angrily.

"Because it happened, of course."

The interrupted vigil

Once a stranger approached a man and demanded that he keep a vigil. When the man asked, "A vigil over what?" the stranger replied, "It makes no difference. Only the vigil matters!"

The man obeyed and sat down to keep vigil. Soon a friend happened by and persuaded him to leave his station. As they walked, the man kept looking over his shoulder.

"What are you doing?" the friend asked.

"Keeping a vigil over my vigil," the man said. "It makes no difference."

The lonely barber

The barber of our town, a lonely man, lived in the basement of the mayor. One Christmas season, while the barber was at work, the mayor's wife and daughter set up a small Christmas tree in the basement and put presents, cookies, and cake under the tree. When the barber came home that night and discovered the tree, he wept for joy. After that, it was noticed in the town that his haircuts began to diminish in quality.

The missing letter

A man receives a letter from his lover. Opening it, he finds nothing inside. Is that itself her message? he wonders. Or did the letter somehow slip out of the envelope? Or did she carelessly forget to insert the letter?

The man keeps the envelope very carefully.

The proper chef and the improper poet

The chef:
"I am happy to be a chef."
"But the rabble complain about your food."
"No. That makes me happy."
The poet:
"I am happy to be a poet."
"But the rabble complain about your poems."
"Yes. That makes me unhappy."

The lonely walking stick

A walking stick, hand-carved by the renowned M. Gunaud, dawdled down a country lane. It was made of the strongest aspen. "The wood of the Cross on Calvary, you know," M. Gunaud, a religious man, often told visitors and friends.

But today he was nowhere to be seen.

A villager approached and said in astonishment, "But where is M. Gunaud?"

The walking stick pointed at the sky. "It looks to rain," he replied, "and M. Gunaud's knees are too painful. He is in the cottage, propped up on pillows, sitting before the fire eating oat cakes and drinking black tea."

"Why did he send you?"

"So that passersby might not forget his pain!"

The villager thought a moment.

"You know, now that you mention it, I do miss M. Gunaud's hobble. It is, you may say, a village treasure. Yet he must be lonely."

"Am *I* not equally lonely?" the walking stick said indignantly, and walked on.

Soon he entered a wood, and the feeling came upon him that the wood, too, was lonely for M. Gunaud's hobble. And the meadow, and the hills, the clouds and mountains in the distance, and finally the world; they, too, were lonely for the hobble. And so, feeling less lonely, the walking stick passed into the world, and never returned to the one who had made him.

The two wayfarers

Once two wayfarers met in a wood, built a fire and spent the night. Before retiring, they asked each other many questions about their past. And with each question their answers always included the words,

"When my mother was alive."

This answer was repeated many times, until they fell asleep. In the morning they parted, satisfied that each had learned all he needed to know about the other's past.

The beam and the sunlight

An errant beam of sunlight lost his way and despaired.
"But all is light here!" the sunlight said.
"I have lost my way," the beam repeated.

The happy petitioner

The court of Judgment Day having convened, the judges said to a petitioner, "You are allowed to judge yourself!"

"Am I, truly?" the astonished and happy petitioner exclaimed. "In that case I have lived an exemplary life and have no regrets!"

"Very well, then. The sentence is passed."

"But what is the sentence?"

"That is the sentence."

The petitioner and the judge

A petitioner complained to a judge about the unfairness of the world.

The judge asked, "Can you measure the unfairness of the world? Can you put a number to it?"

"But of course not!"

"Then the world has treated you fairly," the judge said, dismissing him.

"That, too, is unfair!"

"I said that the world has treated you fairly," the judge replied sternly. "I said nothing about myself."

The honest man

Is honesty truly the best policy?

An honest man was asked,
"What might a personal God look like?"
"Myself, of course!" he replied.
"And what might a personal God not look like?"
"My neighbor, of course!"
"So what might the true God look like?"
"You lay traps for me, my friend, but I have one for you. The true God might look like the true God."
"Who, then, is the true God?"
"The God who commands me to love my neighbor as myself."

The flies and the honeypot

Is death not to be feared after all?

Two flies buzzed around a honeypot, when one flew in.
"How is it with you?" the other fly inquired, hovering.
"As you see," the trapped fly said. "The sweetness . . ."
"But how is it *truly* with you?"
"Well," the dying fly said, "all I can tell you is, it really isn't so bad."
The other fly hovered, wings suddenly weary, dreaming of sweetness. . . .

The eloquent mime

As everyone knows, the mime entertains the crowd by allowing them to see what they wish in the mime's silence, so that, as one might say, the mime *is* his silence.

"And what does the mime say to you?" one member of the crowd asks another.

"I see no mime."

The courting butterflies

Is it necessary to know in order to love?

In a deep forest a beautiful flower grew next to a dull gray rock. To pass the long hours, they were in the habit of conversing about everything under the sun and moon.

One day a pair of courting butterflies fluttered by; the first lighted on the gray rock, the second on the beautiful flower.

"You flatter me," said the rock to the first butterfly.

"Thank you," the first butterfly said.

"You flatter *me*," the second butterfly said to the flower.

"Thank you," said the flower.

After a time, the butterflies fluttered off, but returned the next day. This time the first butterfly lighted on the flower, the second on the rock.

"You flatter me," the flower said to the first butterfly.

"Thank you," said the butterfly.

"You flatter *me*," said the second butterfly to the rock.

"Thank you," said the rock.

Whereupon the courting butterflies, their ardor cooled, fluttered off, never to speak again. And the rock and the flower continued the conversation as before.

The short-sighted travelers

Is mastery of one's moods a good thing? Is slavery to one's moods a good thing?

Two men met in a country inn. Now it happened that one was a slave to his moods, the other a master of his moods. They ate and drank long into the night, until both, as you would expect, wound up envying the other.

One said,

"My friend, seeing that you are a slave to your moods cheers me up, because you are always surprised by life; for you there's always something new around the corner!"

The other said,

"My friend, seeing that you are a master of your moods cheers me up as well, because you can always dictate how you feel, never falling into moments of delirious joy, where one may drop one's guard; or into moments of deep sorrow, where one is a danger to oneself!"

And the two men, having cheered each other up, went on their way.

The claque

Is deception a higher form of truth?

A claque is a group of people hired to applaud a play and turn it into a success.[4] On one occasion in our town, in spite of a strenuous, hard-clapping and loud-whistling claque in the first three rows, a play failed miserably. But since the claque was so convincing, even though the play was not, the audience enthusiastically begged them to come up on stage and continue their own performance, which, in the long run, was more successful than the play. . . .

4. A better contemporary analogy = canned laughter.

The mistletoe and the street

Her eyes sparkled as she expressed childlike delight in the cardinals, yellow finches, hawks, and Huntington's quail flying about in our desert neighborhood. That was the last time I saw this beautiful nineteen-year-old girl; less than a year later she was living on the streets somewhere in Indiana—to be discovered by another street person, no doubt, even as I'd discovered her under a mesquite tree dripping with mistletoe, the Golden Bough of Greek mythology.

Goddesses make their own importance.[5]

---

5. This actually happened to me, proving, I suppose, that on occasion reality and parable may be one and the same. Kafka writes,

> Many complain that the words of the wise are always merely parables and of no use in daily life, which is the only life we have. When the sage says: 'Go over,' he does not mean that we should cross to some actual place, which we could do anyhow if the labor were worth it; he means some fabulous wonder, something unknown to us, something too that he cannot designate more precisely, and therefore cannot help us here in the very least. All these parables really set out to say merely that the incomprehensible is incomprehensible, and we know that already. But the cares we have to struggle with every day: that is a different matter.
>
> Concerning this a man once said: Why such reluctance? If you only followed the parables you yourself would become parables and with that rid of all your daily cares.
>
> Another said: I bet that is also a parable.
>
> The first said: You have won.
>
> The second said: But unfortunately only in parable.
>
> The first said: No, in reality: in parable you have lost.

The parrot with smoker's cough

Is "the real thing" truly real?

A very old woman, owner of a very young green and yellow parrot, had a severe smoker's cough, which the parrot gaily imitated day and night. Eventually, however, and for reasons unknown, the very young parrot died and the very old owner lived on.

The rope

"A poor fellow went to hang himself, but finding by chance a hidden pot containing money, flung away the rope, and went merrily home; but he that had hidden the money, when he found it had been removed by someone, hanged himself with the rope the other man had left behind."[6]

Don't hide your money; invest it in the man who manufactures rope.

6. Ausonious (2nd century A.D.)

Jesus's bitter tears

Lazarus of Bethany, risen from the dead, walked the dusty streets as before. Word had spread about Jesus's miracle, and a crowd of townspeople gathered around him.

"Behold Lazarus, risen from the dead," some shouted, and began to mock him. Among the crowd were disbelievers who claimed that Lazarus hadn't died at all, and that Jesus had performed a trick. Others more kindly implored Lazarus to speak of the afterlife.

"I am forbidden to do so," Lazarus said.

"Well, what can you tell us?"

"Jesus has known sin!" Lazarus said.

The crowd stirred angrily.

"Let Lazarus die a second time," they said, and picked up stones. And yet they were afraid.

"What are you waiting for?" Lazarus sneered. "*I* am not afraid. I shall be twice blessed!"

"Twice blessed?" the crowd repeated Lazarus's words, whispering and staring.

The townspeople of Bethany dropped their stones, and fell on their knees before Lazarus, as the man who held the key to the mystery, not of death, but of life.

And Jesus, when he learned of Lazarus's words, wept for the townspeople of Bethany.

The angry boy

Is anger the object of its own disaffection?

A man, who as a small boy had witnessed the death of his father, was reminiscing with an old family friend.

"Do you remember," the man asked the friend, "the time you took us neighborhood kids on a hike in the hills above Mill Valley?"

"I do," the friend nodded. "Someone brought streamers made of red and gold crepe paper, and you children ran up and down the hills, trying to fly them like kites. But what I remember in particular was how angry *you* seemed; you kept using words I never thought I'd hear from a boy that age."

The man leaned forward. "And of course that was after my father died."

"No, no; before."

"Before!" the man exclaimed. "My father was still alive?"

"Your father was still alive."

The man sat back, speechless; for he had always assumed. . . .Then, remembering the father, his mind clouded over, and the man felt once again that strange rage toward the father, that he had died, leaving the boy behind so many years ago.

The impromptu drummer

A friend invites a man to attend a band rehearsal. During the break, the man, who has never in his life held drumsticks, walks on stage and drums magnificently—everyone at the practice is amazed and applauds lustily. Then the drummer returns and takes back the sticks, and the man leaves the stage, knowing in his heart that he will never be able to drum again without a drummer to return and take back the sticks.

The chess players

Does the word inspire the truth? Or does the truth inspire the word?

Two men sat at a chessboard. Tired of playing, and casting about for a topic of conversation, they began to talk about trust.

"You cannot have trust without mistrust," one proposed, "because mistrust is what gives trust meaning."

"Granted," the other said, sitting back in his chair. "But that means there really is no such thing as trust, for the fear of mistrust always lurks in the shadows."

"But there are those who trust."

"Yes, of course; but as we know, they are the ones most likely to be betrayed."

"Mistrust, then was, as you might say, the serpent in the Garden."

"No, no; trust was the serpent in the Garden."

"Then there were two serpents."

The other was silent.

"I trust we agree?"

The other still looked doubtful.

"You can trust me," the first smiled. "There were two serpents."

"Then I *cannot* trust you."

"Exactly!" the first said in triumph. "We do agree."

And so, trusting each other, they resumed the game of chess, watching each other's moves very carefully.

The philosopher's false words

Does wisdom improve?

A philosopher[7] once wrote,

"Everything is at its peak of perfection. This is especially true of the art of making one's way in the world. There is more required nowadays to make a single wise person than formerly to make the Seven Sages of ancient Greece, and more is needed nowadays to deal with a single person than was required with a whole people in former times."

"Gracian is wrong," one man said to another, who had just read these words aloud. "Everything is at its peak of imperfection. There is less required nowadays to make a single wise person, and less is needed to deal with a single person."

"That is wise" the other nodded in agreement. "But what was required for you to summon the wisdom to refute Gracian's words?"

---

7. Baltasar Gracian.

The men at table

What is a fool?

Two men sat at table drinking wine. One proposed,

"A fool may have character, but not intellect."

"No, no," the other disagreed. "A fool may easily have intellect. Look at the state of our universities!"

"Then let me pose you a question," the first said, picking up a book. He read out loud,

"'Intellect is not enough, character is also needed. On the other hand, it is the fool's misfortune to fail in obtaining the position, employment, neighborhood, and circle of friends of his choice.'"

He closed the book.

"Now," he resumed, "in speaking of the fool, is the philosopher[8] talking about character or intellect?"

"Neither," the other said.

---

8. Gracian.

The immortal things of this world

How may one speak of death and immortality in the same breath?

Two philosophers sat at table drinking wine and eating cheese.

"We don't agree on much, my friend," one said. "But will you agree that there are things in life that do not change; that they are, I mean to say, immortal?"

"Yes."

"And will you also agree that the immortal things of this world cannot bestow immortality?"

"Yes, my friend. That is why they are immortal!"

Second parable of the men at table

What is the role of Necessity when justice and free will are eternally at loggerheads?

Two philosophers sat at table drinking wine and eating cheese. One said,

"You will agree that free will and justice have nothing to do with each other, and that in fact they are at loggerheads as often as not?"

"Yes, I agree. Free will is free will, just or not."

"No, no, my friend; *not* 'just or not'; they are two separate things. Free will must make its way in the world independent of justice."

"Then it is just, I suppose, that free will should do so."

"Yes; I grant you that."

"But have I not caught you in a trap?"

"No, my friend. I grant you that because I must."

Of love

A man sat down by the sea. Soon a wave rose up, crashed on the sand before him, and flung a single drop into his hand. Looking at it he thought, as many men would, that the entire sea was contained in that drop—the proportion of salt to water, even a tiny fleck of foam.

Then, as the wave receded, and still holding the drop in his hand, he tore off his clothes and gave himself to the sea.

The thumbscrew

Two philosophers sat at table drinking wine and eating cheese.

"Every man has a thumbscrew, my friend," one observed.

"Yes," the other agreed. And they began to speak of a third man, who was not present.

"And what is his thumbscrew?"

"Loneliness."

"And what is it that applies the thumbscrew?"

"Love, as you know, my friend."

Then they began to speak of a fourth man.

"And what is his thumbscrew?"

"Love."

"And what is it that applies the thumbscrew?"

"Loneliness, as you know, my friend."

"We are speaking of the same person, are we not?"

The beautiful hair

Two men walked in the woods. One asked the other,

"My friend, is there nothing more beautiful in the world than a woman letting down her hair?"

"I prefer to watch a woman putting up her hair," the other replied. "Nothing in the world more beautiful than that."

"No matter," the first man nodded. "We are speaking of the same woman!"

"No, no," the other protested. "Two different women."

"Cannot the same woman be as beautiful letting down and putting up her hair?"

"My friend, you do not know women."

"And you, my friend, do not know men."

The unhappy couple

A man and a woman disputed long and bitterly into the night. Finally the man said,

"I demand that you tell me whether or not you love me."

She thought a moment.

"No," she said, "I do not."

He thought a moment.

"You made that decision long ago!" he accused.

"Yes," she admitted. "But I did not realize that I had made it until just now."

The mystery of heroes

Is heroism revenge?

Two men walked in the street. One said,

"Alas, there are no more heroes in the world."

"You are quite wrong, my friend," the other said. "One sees a hero everywhere one looks."

"Surely you are too easily impressed," the first said, and pointed to a mutual acquaintance walking ahead of them. "Is *he* a hero?"

"Yes, my friend. He hates his work, yet does it well; better, perhaps, than if he loved it. It is, as you might say, his revenge."

The flowering tree[9]

Two birds perched on the branch of a flowering tree. One ate of the fruit, the other looked at it.

"Verily, we are of one soul," said one. "I look at the fruit, you eat of it."

"No, no; we are of two souls," said the other.

"Then you have no need of me!" said the bird who looked at the fruit, and flew off.

And the bird that stayed on the branch grew lean and gaunt, for he no longer wished to eat.

9. Improvisation on an Upanishad.

The reluctant pallbearer

Is a small measure of comfort truly better than none at all?

Two friends were walking in the woods when one suddenly stopped.

"I can't move," he announced. "I can't go forward or backward. You must carry me."

The other picked up his friend, carried him home, and put him to bed. The next day, when the friend still could not move, the other summoned a doctor, who announced that he could do nothing. From then on, day after day, year after year, the other carried his friend wherever he needed to go. Then, in extreme old age, as the other carried his friend through the woods, the friend announced, "I can move. You may put me down." The other put him down, but, on returning home, the friend collapsed and died.

The other dutifully arranged for the funeral, but when it came time to appoint pallbearers, he refused to include himself, asking six other men to do the job.

And in walking behind the six men as they carried the coffin through the streets to the cemetery, the other took a small measure of comfort.

The matador

Are miracles what we truly desire?

Once a matador found that he had the wonderful ability to allow the charging bull to pass through his body, as though it weren't there! This maddened the bull, but, of course, delighted and amazed the crowd, who cheered and threw flowers. But soon the flowers turned to cushions, the traditional sign of disapproval; for the crowd had grown tired of seeing the bull pass through the matador's body, while the matador took no risks. Finally the matador begged to be restored to flesh and bone. The wish was granted, and the bulls and the crowd were satisfied.

The wild card

May the wild card be anything but another card?

Once a man was born as a wild card—that is, a person who could be anyone he wished. But, of course, that meant he was no one at all, and so he passed through life becoming this soul and that soul until, wearily, he lay on his deathbed.

But his friends saw that the man was smiling.

"Why, you die happy after all!" they exclaimed.

"Yes," the man said. "I have become so accustomed to being a wild card that I have become a wild card and nothing else."

The man died, still smiling.

The man in search of Evil

Once a man went in search of Evil, but Evil mysteriously eluded him. He sought out the loose women of the town in order to be unfaithful to his wife, but the women shook their heads.

"Go back to your wife," they said.

Then he attempted to become a thief, but his victims smiled and took pity and willingly gave him their possessions, saying, "It is not in you to be a thief, my friend." Thus the man went through life, day after day, year after year, in an unsuccessful search for Evil. When he died, he came before God and hung his head.

"Look up, man!" God commanded. "Verily, hath the Good not prevailed?"

Thus it was God punished him by sending him to heaven.

The man with no illusions

Two men were strolling in a meadow when one announced that he had no illusions.
"But that itself is an illusion," the other said. "We all have illusions, my friend!"
"That, too, is an illusion," said the first.
"Then Everything is an illusion!"
"No, no, my friend," the first replied, "Nothing is an illusion!"
"But that is the same thing!"
The first nodded in agreement, and they strolled on.

The tender seamstress

May the moment of death change everything in life?

A seamstress made beautiful quilts, giving them away far and wide. All she asked of her beneficiaries was, "Treat my quilts with utmost tenderness."

But one beneficiary used her quilt to cover sensitive plants in her garden during cold weather, and soon it was ruined. Another placed it on the bed, but the family dogs ripped it to shreds. Still another placed it on the bed as well, but soon tore it up for rags.

So it went, until the seamstress died, and her friends brought one of her quilts to lay on her coffin. "Remember," one said, "we must treat the quilt with utmost tenderness." And they did.

The man with the superior gait

Is it better to be remembered for a trifle than for nothing at all?

Once a man possessed a certain way of walking, an attractive gait that turned heads wherever he went. He became known as "The Man with the Superior Gait," and, understanding this, he walked everywhere, shunning the horse and carriage.

When he died, he was buried under a tombstone which memorialized his gait. And in the eyes of the world, he was remembered with the admiration and esteem that was once accorded a man of noble heart.

Improvisations on Aesop's Fables

The dog and the ox

Once upon a time a mean-spirited dog went to rest in a manger. When the tired and hungry ox came in from the field and wanted to eat his hay, the dog barked at him fiercely, even though he had no wish to eat the hay himself. But the ox, seeing that he was much larger than the dog, sat on him and enjoyed the hay.

The next time you see an ox, think twice about barking.

The goose and the golden eggs

Once upon a time a man had a goose that laid a golden egg each day. Although he was becoming rich, he grew impatient. Wishing to have the treasure all at once, he killed the goose. Cutting open the goose, however, the man found her just like any other, but she made such fine eating that, upon devouring her in a single meal, he said "Oh, well," and in the end was happy for the golden eggs that he already had.

A full belly and gratitude go together well.

The dog and his shadow

A dog, carrying a piece of meat in his mouth, was crossing a stream on a narrow foot-bridge. He happened to look into the water and saw his shadow, but he thought it was another dog with a piece of meat larger than his. He made a grab for the other dog's meat, but in doing so he dropped his own meat, lost his balance, fell into the water, and drowned.

The punishment doesn't always fit the crime.

The merchant and the statue of Hermes

A man of the country carved a wooden statue of the god Hermes and carried it to the market to offer it for sale, but no buyer came along. So the man began telling the crowd that he was selling a god who would be of great help around the house and in the fields.

A man heard these words and said to the merchant,

"Friend, we are not as foolish as you suppose. If the wooden god is so helpful around the house and in the fields, why are you selling him rather than using him yourself?"

"Oh, but I *am* using him," the merchant assured the man. "I am just giving him a little help, for you know what they say, 'The gods help those who help the gods!'"

And the man bought the statue.

Sometimes it's better to get it backward.

The farmer and the eagle

In the ancient days an old farmer, known far and wide for dishonesty and meanness of heart, caught an eagle in the fields. He clipped its wings and released it into the barnyard to live in shame and humiliation with the poultry, who, of course, mocked him.

Then another man came along and bought the eagle. Taking pity on the great bird, he rubbed its wings with myrrh until they grew again. And the eagle swooped into the air as before.

Soon the eagle spotted a hare, swooped down, caught it, and decided to offer it to the man who had bought him as a gift. And a fox who saw what had happened said,

"My friend, you should not give the hare to this man. You should give it to the old farmer to deter him from catching you and clipping your wings again."

The eagle sought out the farmer and offered the hare to him. And the farmer took the hare, clipped the eagle's wings again, and put him back in the barnyard, where the eagle lived in shame and humiliation until the end of his days.

1. Deterrence doesn't always work, in the barnyard and in many other places. 2. If you don't want your wings clipped, learn the difference between deterrence and appeasement.

The farmer, the Cyclops, and the gold

In the land of the Cyclops, where Odysseus and his crew once visited, there was a prosperous farmer who lived with his wife and sons amid rich fields of wheat and barley. In time, however, the farmer's fortunes changed, the rains did not come, and he fell into despair. Deciding to kill himself, he took his sword into the fields, whereupon he happened upon a cache of gold left behind by a passing Cyclops. He threw down the sword, stuffed the gold in his pockets, and went home full of joy.

Soon thereafter the Cyclops returned for his gold. Seeing that it was missing, he fell into despair, picked up the sword left by the farmer, and plunged it into his breast!

If you don't keep an eye on your money, you deserve what you get.

The debtor, the creditor, and the enchanted sow

A creditor demanded that a debtor pay his debt; the debtor said he could not, but offered to sell his sow, which he claimed was enchanted, to the first man who came along. When a farmer happened by, the debtor asked if he would buy the enchanted sow, and the farmer asked if she were fertile.

"Oh, yes," the debtor assured him. "During the winter festival of the Eleusinian mysteries she gave birth to males, and during the summer festival of Zeus she gave birth to females!"

"Hah!" the creditor interrupted. "This is much too fantastic. Next you will tell him that the sow would give birth to baby goats for the god Dionysius."

The debtor thought a moment, for the creditor had given him an idea.

"No," he said to the creditor, "but she will give birth to debtors!"

And the creditor took the sow and forgave the debtor's debt.

Greed is defined as interest charged on creditors.

The loquacious cat and the clever cock

A cat caught a cock in its claws.

"I'm going to eat you because you keep people awake with your infernal crowing," said the cat.

"No, no," countered the cock. "Thanks to the likes of me the farmer performs his chores on time."

"Well," said the cat, "I am going to eat you because you live in sin with your mother and sisters."

"Yes," admitted the cock, "but that is how chickens provide eggs for the farmer."

So it went, accusation after accusation, justification after justification, until the cat, weakened with hunger, fainted dead away and the cock escaped to live another day.

Don't talk with your mouth empty.

The fox and the henhouse

A fox, hearing that some chickens were sick, put on a doctor's white coat, found a doctor's black bag, and visited the henhouse.

Immediately the cock guarding the henhouse threw him out.

"Go work your mischief in another henhouse!" the cock called after him.

"Congratulations," said a clever hen to the cock, "You saved us from the fox!"

"Fox?" said the astonished cock, "I thought he was a doctor!"

Even foxes don't make house calls.

The donkey and the magic potion

A donkey, weary of turning a millstone around and around, pretended to have an attack of epilepsy in order to get some rest. Its owner called in an apothecary, who said,

"I have a magic potion that you can administer to the donkey. He'll be up and around in no time!"

But when the owner administered the potion, it did not agree with the donkey, and the poor creature died!

Even an ass should know that epilepsy is a disease, not a cure.

The master, the ugly slave-girl, and Aphrodite

A certain master loved an ugly slave-girl who worked in his house. But the slave-girl was not satisfied to be loved, and she prayed to Aphrodite to make her beautiful so that the master would love her even more.

Now the presumption of the slave-girl irritated the jealous Aphrodite, who was also angry at the master for preferring the ugly slave-girl to her. And so, to take revenge on them both, the goddess granted her wish and made her beautiful! And the master, seeing that she was no longer the ugly slave-girl he loved, cast her out of his house, and lived alone to the end of his days.

Ugly, too, is in the eye of the beholder.

The partridge and the cocks

A man caught a partridge and brought it home. When he put it in the same pen with his cocks, they pecked and tormented her, until she despaired of being wrongly discriminated against as an inferior member of a different race.

Then she noticed that the cocks also pecked and tormented each other, and she said to herself, "What a relief! These inferior cocks have no mercy on each other either!"

1. Prejudice is a double-edged sword grasped by the blade. 2. You can have your cake of political correctness and eat it too.

The hungry fisherman and the small mackerel

A hungry fisherman cast his nets in the sea but caught only one small mackerel. The fish begged for its life, saying, "If you let me go I will grow up to be a very large fish, and you can catch me then, and I will feed you and your family for many days."

But the fisherman said to the small mackerel, "If I let you go, I may never see you again, no matter how big you are when you grow up!" And he took the mackerel home, and his wife scolded him as always, and the fisherman and his family again went hungry.

A large mackerel in the sea is worth more than a small mackerel in the hand.

The fisherman and the stranger

A fisherman cast his nets across a river, damming it up. Then he beat on the water, so that the fish would become afraid and swim into the net. A stranger appeared and said to the fisherman,

"If you keep beating the water, it will become muddied, and we who live in the vicinity will not be able to drink."

But the fisherman said, "If I stop beating the water, I will go hungry."

To die of thirst or of hunger, what does it matter?

The mule and the race

A mule was feeling full of pride and thought, "My father is a fast-running horse, and I take after him!" The mule entered a race, but at the last minute the father decided to enter too, and won the race. "Oh, well," the mule acknowledged, "I was merely lying to myself, for my father is really an ass."

Lest you make an ass of yourself, don't depend on your father to fight your battles.

The gnat, the lion, and the spider

Once upon a time a gnat said to a lion, "You are much bigger than I am, but I'll wager I can outfight you!"

"Done!" said the lion, and he prepared for battle. But the gnat flew into the lion's nose and began biting him and biting him, until the lion clawed at himself frantically, causing much pain and loss of blood. Finally the poor lion ran away.

Then the gnat, puffed up with pride, flew around the forest, bragging of his prowess. But he grew careless and landed in a spider's web. As he was about to be devoured, the gnat lamented,

"Woe is me, that I, the new king of beasts, should have been brought to such a pass by an ordinary spider!"

It takes two to weave a web of deception.

The wolf and the ewe

Once upon a time a wolf happened upon a ewe, who immediately began shivering with fright.

"Don't worry, my dear," the wolf said, "If you tell me one truth, I will spare you."

"Very well," the ewe said. "Wolves are not to be trusted."

Enraged, the wolf devoured the ewe.

It takes two to bear witness to the truth: one to utter it, the other to turn a deaf ear.

The seagull and the kite

Once upon a time a seagull swallowed a fish for dinner, but the fish got caught in its gullet. The unfortunate gull died, and its ghost flew to the Underworld. Then a kite happened by, saw the seagull's body lying on the beach, and said,

"Serves you right, my friend! You were a bird, and you should have earned your living on land, not in the sea!"

Just then a succulent young crab came out of the sea onto the land, and the kite, unable to resist, devoured it. His gullet, too, burst, and the ghost followed the seagull's ghost down to the Underworld.

And there the seagull and the kite bickered for all eternity about who got what he deserved, and why!

The next time someone tells you that the world is governed by poetic justice, don't quarrel; just let it go, even as the seagull and the kite should've let go of their catches.

The vixen and the lioness

Once upon a time a vixen haughtily criticized a lioness for having only one child.

"It is true that I have just one," replied the lioness equally haughtily, "but he is a lion nonetheless!"

Always take quality over quantity, except in the case of only children, who, often as not, are spoiled rotten.

The lion and the fox

Once upon a time an old, sick lion had to resort to trickery to obtain his food. Remaining in his cave, he promised the animals a hearty dinner if they would enter. When they entered, he kept his promise by eating them for dinner! But, lions being what they are, he was never satisfied.

Then a fox happened by, but hesitated. The lion said, "Why not come in for dinner, my friend?"

The fox said, "I would do so, except that I see that the footprints of my brethren lead in to your cave, but none lead out!"

The lion thought a moment; then he said,

"But would you enter if the footprints led out of the cave as well?"

"No, no, that would not at all be satisfactory!" exclaimed the fox. "For clearly it would mean that your company is not worth keeping!"

Avoid the company of those who are never satisfied.

The ploughman and the lion

Once upon a time a ploughman left his barn door open and a lion sneaked in. He commenced to eat the sheep, oxen, and cattle that lived in the barn.

The ploughman's wife was beside herself and shouted at her husband,

"This is a fine state of affairs! What do you plan to do with the lion once he has eaten all of our livestock?"

"No, my dear," said the ploughman, "the question is, what does the lion plan to do with us?"

The essence of folly is to plan ahead too late.

The lion and the dull-witted ploughman's daughter

Once upon a time a lion fell in love with the daughter of a dull-witted ploughman, and asked for her hand in marriage. Afraid of the prospect of having such a ferocious son-in-law, the ploughman told the lion he would grant his request if he would consent to having his teeth and claws removed. The lion agreed, but once the operation was performed, the ploughman told him to go back to where he came from.

"But why do you send me away?" asked the lion.

"It just now occurred to me," answered the ploughman, "what on earth would the children of a marriage between a lion and a girl look like?"

It's all right to be slow on the uptake with a lion, providing that it has no claws or teeth.

The lion, the bear, and the fox

Once upon a time a bear and a lion fought over the carcass of a faun in the forest. They exchanged many blows to the head and face, until finally both of them dizzily collapsed. A fox happened by, saw the faun and the two fighters lying on their backs, and took the faun, saving it for a tasty supper.

The bear said to the lion, "Woe is us, to have gone through all of this just to feed a fox!"

Then the lion said to the bear, "But this has given me new strength! Let's go after the fox."

And, reinvigorated, the bear and the lion chased after the fox, caught him, and enjoyed the fox and the faun for supper.

Deadly easy to outfox a punch-drunk bear and a punch-drunk lion.

The lion, the fox, and the stag

Once upon a time a sick and ageing lion asked the fox, his neighbor, to induce a stag to come to his cave, for he could no longer hunt as he did when younger. "I have wanted to devour a stag for a long time," said the lion, "especially the heart!"

The fox went into the forest, found a stag drinking at a pool, and told him that the lion lay ill and dying and wished to anoint the stag the new king of animals. The stag, puffed up with pride, agreed to accompany the fox back to the lion's cave, whereupon the lion managed to seize him and eat his entrails and bones, even the marrow; but the heart fell to the floor of the cave. The fox, seeing the heart, devoured it himself, thinking it just compensation for the errand he had run for the lion.

The lion, still hungry, asked the fox what happened to the heart.

"But the stag had no heart, your majesty," said the fox in a trembling voice. "How could an animal be said to have a heart that was foolish enough to enter a lion's den under such a flimsy pretext?"

"You're talking about the brains, you fool, not the heart!" said the lion, and devoured the fox in one piece.

Show me a fox that flunks Anatomy 101 and I'll show you a fox with no anatomy at all.

The frog, the lion, and Zeus

Once upon a time a lion heard a frog croaking loudly in the woods. Thinking that the frog was as large as he, the lion approached the pond where the frog lived, but, seeing that he was so small, caught him and crushed him.

"Such loud noises from one so very small!" the lion roared.

Then Zeus, seeing what had happened, strode across the mountains and crushed the lion.

"Such loud noises from one so very small," Zeus said.

Frogs and lions would do better to keep their own counsel.

The lion and the wild boar

A lion and a wild boar went down to a spring to drink. Since there wasn't enough water for both of them, they decided to have a contest of strength to see which could vanquish the other. The competition began, and they struggled and struggled, but soon noticed that vultures had gathered nearby to see who would win. Then the lion said to the boar, "This is silly. Better that we become friends than become food for vultures!"

What matters isn't whether you win or lose but how you play the game.

The lion and the dolphin

Once upon a time a lion went down to the seashore. He told a passing dolphin, "You and I should be friends, for I am king of beasts on the land and you are king of beasts in the sea!"

"Very well, my friend," agreed the dolphin.

Time passed, and the lion returned to the shore.

"I need your help," he said to the dolphin, "for a wild bull has picked me to be his enemy."

"Friend, I cannot walk on the land," said the dolphin. "Besides, a whale has picked me to be his enemy."

"Bah!" said the lion. "Let me demonstrate to you that we *can* help one another." And he leaped in the waves, intent on pursuing the whale, but drowned!

Better to know your friends than to be picked by your enemies.

About the Author

In 2005 Steven Carter retired as Emeritus Professor of English after teaching in the university for thirty-eight years. The author of thirteen books published here and abroad, he served as Senior Fulbright Fellow at two Polish universities in 1991. He is the only two-time winner of Italy's coveted *Nuove Lettere* International Poetry and Literature Prize. Carter and his wife Janice divide the year between Arizona and Montana.

www.ingramcontent.com/pod-product-compliance
Lightning Source LLC
Chambersburg PA
CBHW081357090726
47908CB00011B/2709

* 9 7 8 0 7 6 1 8 4 8 2 0 2 *